T0309674

Being a Skull

Georges Didi-Huberman

Being a Skull

Site, Contact, Thought, Sculpture

Translated by Drew S. Burk

Être crâne: Lieu, Contact, Pensée, Sculpture
by Georges Didi-Huberman
© Les Éditions de Minuit, 7, rue Bernard-Palissy, 75006

Translated by Drew S. Burk
as *Being a Skull: Site, Contact, Thought, Sculpture*

Published by Univocal
411 N Washington Ave, STE 10
Minneapolis, MN 55401
English Language Edition © Univocal

Special thanks go to Georges Didi-Huberman,
Lia Mitchell, and Jon Thrower

Cet ouvrage, publié dans le cadre d'un programme d'aide à la publication,
bénéficie du soutien de l'Institut Français et de la Mission Culturelle et
Universitaire Française aux Etats-Unis, service de la France aux Etats-Unis.

This work, published as part of a program of aid for publication, received
support from the Institut Français and the Mission Culturelle et Universitaire
Française aux Etats-Unis, a department of the French Embassy in the
United States.

Cover Design by Jason Wagner
adapted from the artwork by Giuseppe Penone,
Landscape of the Brain, 1990

Distributed by the University of Minnesota Press

ISBN 9781937561703
Library of Congress Control Number: 2016950169

Table of Contents

Hors crâne seul dedans
quelque part quelquefois
comme quelque chose

crâne abri dernier
pris dans le dehors […]

Outside skull alone inside
some where some time
as some thing

skull shelter terminal
caught within the outside […]

Samuel Beckett, *Poèmes*
(Paris: Minuit, 1978)

Being a Box

So as not to feel too obstinately gazed upon by the hollowed out orbits of the human skull before him, the scientist of bodies — the anatomist — always prefers, as is well known, to speak of the cranial box. Paul Richer, Charcot's collaborator at la Salpêtrière hospital as well as professor of anatomy at the École des Beaux-Arts — who had as part of his work under these two professional titles, both to describe malformations and symptomatic ugliness as well as prescribe "correct forms" and ideal beauty — presented, to his audience full of future prize-winning art students, the morphology of the human skull in the following manner: "The cranium is a sort of bony box, irregularly ovoid in shape. It stands at the top of the vertebral canal and opens into it. In fact, it has quite correctly been regarded as an enlargement of the vertebral canal. The cranium encloses the brain, just as the vertebral column encloses the spinal cord, which is itself but an extension of the brain."[1]

After this useful reminder — so as to not completely omit what the skull encases, namely the encephalon, our organ for thought — Paul Richer could then undertake the desired

---

1. Paul Richer, *Artistic Anatomy*, trans. Robert Beverly Hale (New York: Watson-Guptill Publications, 1971), 21.

systematic and exhaustive description of the cranial anatomy: the exhaustion system does nothing more than follow with complete confidence the trivial topology of a box, that is, a regular volume endowed with six sides, successively named "anterior aspect," "[two] lateral aspects," "superior aspect," "posterior aspect," and "inferior aspect (the base of the skull)"[2] (figs. 1-4). So, here we indeed have something that, as they say, is common sense: in order to completely describe the cranial box, is it not enough to simply turn around it in order to exhaust the totality of its "aspects," as Richer so perfectly states? But what is often considered to be "common sense," also leads one to encounter little subjective moments of forgetting, of repression or denial of a primary disturbance or concern whose descriptive or objective attention merely provides a convenient guardrail.

Confronted with his cranial *box*, Paul Richer simply forgot the question that every magic box, that every case for a precious item, or every concave organ, or vital place poses: the question of the interior, the question of folds. It is significant that, within the formulation itself of the title of his work, anatomy was qualified as being "artistic" for the reason that the forms described were reduced to the "exterior forms" — we can almost hear within this phrase "presentable forms" — of the human body. But if the skull is a box, then it's Pandora's box: to truly open it would be to unleash all the "beautiful evils," all the anxieties and concerns of a thought that would turn around its own destiny, its own folds, its own *place*. To open this box is to also risk plunging into it, to risk losing one's head, to risk — from the inside — being devoured.

---

2. Ibid., 139–140.

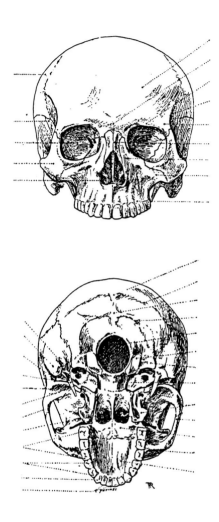

Fig. 1. Richer, "The Skull, Anterior Aspect," *Artistic Anatomy*, 139.
Fig. 2. "The Skull, Inferior Aspect, Base of Cranium," ibid., 140.

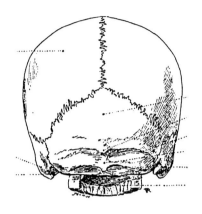

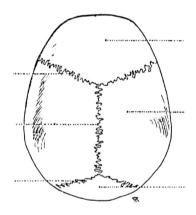

Fig. 3. "The Skull, Posterior Aspect, Base of Cranium," ibid.
Fig. 4. "The Skull, Superior Aspect," ibid.

Being an Onion

Leonardo da Vinci (who, it goes without saying, is much less of an academic artist than Paul Richer) also described and drew the human skull. But he did so following a completely different intention and attention: in his work, the forms in play don't need to be "presentable forms," and the descriptive planes are never envisioned from their "respectable distances." Da Vinci likes to get close to and even penetrate inside the object of his curiosity (figs. 5–6). What first of all fascinates him, inside the human skull, is what he names the "internal side"; it's the "orbitals' cavities," with their hidden "depth"; in general, it's all those "visible holes" as well as those that are harder to see than the canals whereby, according to him, tears directly rise from the heart all the way toward the eyes.[3]

---

3. "I wish to elevate that part of the bone, the support of the cheek, which is found between the 4 lines a b c d, and to demonstrate through the exposed opening the size and depth of the two cavities which are hidden behind it. The eye, the instrument of vision, is hidden in the cavity above, and in that below is the humor which nourishes the roots of the teeth. The cavity of the cheekbone has a resemblance in depth and size to the cavity which receives the eye within it, and in capacity it is very similar to it and receives in its interior some veins through the opening m, which descend from the brain, passing through the sieve (chocolatorio) [*ethmoid*] which discharges into the nose the superfluities of the humors of the head. No other obvious openings are found in the above cavity which surrounds the eye. The opening b [*optic foramen*] is where the visual power passes to the sensorium and the opening n [*nasolacrimal*] is where the tears well up from the heart to the eye, passing through the canal of the nose." Leonardo da Vinci, "The Skull: lateral view," in *Leonardo da Vinci and the Human Body*, edited and translated by Charles

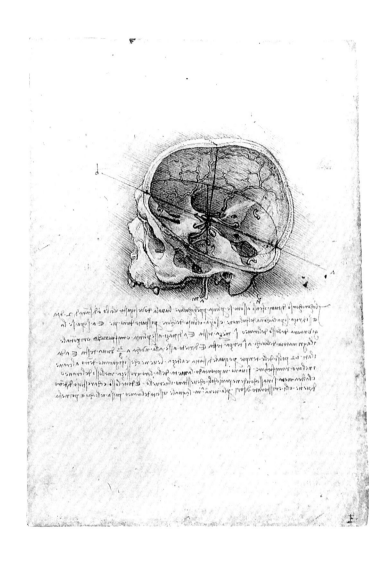

D. O'Malley and J. B. de C. M. Saunders (New York: Crown, 1982), 46. Brackets in O'Malley and Saunders.

"The cavity of the orbit and the cavity of the bone which supports the cheek, and that of the nose and of the mouth, are of equal depth and terminate in a perpendicular line below the sensus communis [*siège des sens*]; and each of these cavities is as long as the third part of a man's face, that is, from the chin to the hair." "Anterior view of the skull with frontal and maxillary sinuses exposed," ibid., 44.

Fig. 5. *(opposite page)* Leonardo da Vinci, "The Skull, Interior View," *The Anatomy of Man: Drawings from the collection of Her Majesty the Queen Elizabeth II* (Houston, TX: Museum of Fine Arts, Houston, 1992), 37.

Fig. 6. Da Vinci, "The Cerebral Ventricles, and the Layers of the Scalp," *Anatomy of Man*, 26.

Another thing also fascinates him: the layered, pellicular, or stratified character of the *system of contact* formed by the bone of the skull and by all that it contains within it — the brain mass, of course, but also the tissues, membranes, humors, or muscles that the skull cloaks and protects, and which serve as interfaces or insulation. An analogy emerges: that of an onion, which da Vinci does not hesitate to draw in front of one of his most famous anatomical cross-sections (fig. 6). An analogy that is so minimally "serious," within the context of a highly "scientific" investigation, that the reproductions of the drawing are sometimes framed so as to get rid of the triviality — the "culinary" side — of this convolution.[4] Da Vinci however is not afraid of counter-signing his drawing with a perfectly explicit text:

> If you cut an onion through the middle, you will be able to see and enumerate all the coats or rinds which circularly clothe the center of this onion. Similarly, if you cut through the middle of the head of a man, you will cut first the hairs, then the scalp, then the muscular flesh [*galea aponeurotica*] and pericranium, then the cranium, and inside the *dura mater*, the *pia mater*, and the brain; then again through the *pia mater* and *dura mater* and *rete mirabile* and then the bone, the foundation.[5]

The onion is not a box. By way of a pellicular paradox, the onion's faculty of containing can be identified exactly with what it contains, which offers — this is certain — an image of predilection for the geometer, the philosopher, and the artist.[6] Indeed, with the onion, the outer skin *is* the core:

4. See notably Martin Kemp, *Leonardo da Vinci: The Miraculous Works of Nature and Man* (Oxford: Oxford University Press, 2006).

5. Leonardo da Vinci, *The Anatomy of Man: Drawings from the collection of Her Majesty the Queen Elizabeth II* (Houston, TX: Museum of Fine Arts, Houston, 1992), 37.

6. See notably Jean Dubuffet, letter to Gaston Chaissac of August 28, 1950, in *Prospectus et tous écrits suivants* vol. II (Paris: Gallimard, 1967), 301: "[…] and once when I wanted to peel an onion I took off the first envelope then the next and so on and so on until I

from then on, there is no longer any possible hierarchy between the center and the periphery. A troubling solidarity, based on contact — but also on infra-thin interstices — unites the envelope with the enveloped thing. Here, the outside is nothing more than *a molting* of the inside. Think of the characteristic trait given within da Vinci's description: the bone, the *pia mater*, and the *dura mater* are successively shown as both the container and the contents. As for the *rete mirabile,* that "admirable rhizome" formed by the encephalon with all its connections, it opens up an area for an organic topology that defies common representation, and for which the skull nevertheless constitutes the geographical site.

---

realized I was going to take off everything and there would be no more onion since an onion is made […] of nothing but successive envelopes that in the end envelop nothing at all. That doesn't stop the onion from being a thing that exists. But peeling it will get you nowhere. […] But then you can say of anything that it's not generally where you're looking for it. Art isn't where you look for it either, but it's there up close right under your nose."

Being a Snail

We generally assume the attention that the Renaissance artists gave to nature — their noted passion for anatomy, perspective, the theory of proportions, etc. — had as its sole purpose the proper reproduction of everything we see surrounding us. But we could say that the opposite is true. Indeed, in many cases, the anatomical *excavation*, the perspectivist *journey*, the *theorization* of forms, provoked nothing but destabilizing consequences: inverted or anni-hilated orientations, visions of things manifesting their strangeness, the never-seen, paradoxes. Whereby the space of familiar visibility becomes distorted and *literally* trans-formed into an *open* site, a site of openness, constructed with the materials of unpredictability and challenges to common sense.

Albrecht Dürer certainly didn't have the same curiosity as da Vinci in regard to the internal forms of the organs — this curiosity that unremittingly digs within the human and creates a whole network of wells, viewpoints, and trenches for the gaze. But for Dürer, form was already an organ, it was already organic — even if it was thought within a strict geometrical framework.[7] Whereas Dürer, right from

---

7. This is perhaps a way of anticipating Goethean morphology (cf. "Morphology" in *Goethe's Botanical Writings* (Woodbridge, Conn: Ox Bow Press, 1989)); and even more

the very first pages of his *Instructions on Measurement*, published in 1525, may very well have begun his study by way of Euclid's "foundations of geometry" — what Dürer embarked upon quickly became a very complex and moving "helical line" — a veritable snail-line, like the spiral of a snail shell (*Schneckelinie*), that he not only then took up sketching, but also began to create and generate by way of a variety of logico-spatial processes (figs. 7–10).[8]

So it was that the passion for morphology opened up unknown worlds, without the necessary tortuous recourse to the systematic dissection of the human head like an onion, as was the case with the explorations of Leonardo da Vinci. When Dürer invented the so-called transfer method, intended to conserve the proportions of one and the same object around which points of view can move — it was not by chance that the chosen example was the human head. With this invention, was Dürer thinking that he was moving within the singular territory of objective observation?

> But there where you would like to sketch out a head portrait according to the logic we have provided, in such a way that the various parts with their profiles and surface areas appear by way of a cross-section of lines, as if the head depicted in the portraiture created though my adventure with wax was in no way cut up by the cross-section of lines which we have demonstrated, will then allow us to know the surface area of the deduction [*retranchement*]: what painters today commonly call inverting the foundations. If you want to undertake it, help yourself to a triangle as I will show you, which we decided

recent morphogenetic perspectives (cf. René Thom's *Semiophysics: A Sketch. Aristotelian Physics and Catastrophe Theory*, trans. Vendla Meyer (Redwood City, CA: Addison-Wesley, 1990). See also Gilbert Chauvet, *The Mathematical Nature of the Living World: The Power of Integration*, (Hackensack, NJ: World Scientific, 2005)).

8. Albrecht Dürer, *The Painter's Manual*, trans. Walter Strauss (New York: Albaris Books, 1977), 50–57.

to call a transfer [*transférant*]: to the extent that what we propose would be capable of being transferred, or otherwise transmuted, in keeping with the logic of proportions […]. By way of this figure, you can discover a diversity of things, which we have depicted [*nous avons portraite*], before demonstrating the means by which it can be accommodated to the inversion of the head which we spoke of (fig. 11).[9]

Perhaps there is, within Dürer's *transfer* method, this "mathematical elucidation" of proportions that Panofsky admired so much.[10] No doubt there is "order" and "reason," which the artist proclaimed loudly and with vigor. But there is indeed something else, we can feel it. Something else that is not the absence of order or reason but rather their *displacement*, their fundamental strangeness. Indeed, what is it to "invert [a head] around its foundation [*fondement*]" as Dürer writes, if not to "invert the foundation of visibility itself?" Namely, to *invert the space* that this visibility admits? Dürer affirms that "inverting the head" helps in "discovering a large diversity of things" — and what he's getting at here is the discovery of unimaginable things before the technical protocol of painting was put into place.

What are these "things"? Unknown "surface areas" and "deductions," where "human" portraiture suddenly becomes inverted, as with the *viewpoint from below* — a humanly impossible point of view, as long as the eye can't view the head from inside the body, unless Dürer holds a cut off head below his eyes — as is demonstrated in a famous drawing from the "Dresden Sketchbook" (fig. 11).

9. Dürer, *Les Quatre Livres d'Albert Dürer, peinctre et géométricien très-excellent: De la proportion et des pourtraicts des corps humains*, translated to French by Loys Meigret Lionnois (Paris: Arnhem chez Jean Jeansz, 1614), http://gallica.bnf.fr/ark:/12148/bpt6k1043173f.

10. Erwin Panofsky, "The History of the Theory of Human Proportions," in *Meaning and the Visual Arts* (Chicago: University of Chicago Press, 1983).

The "mathematical elucidation" will give way to the unrestricted emergence of organic abysses, snail-spaces, and impossible points of view. From then on, in contrast to an anthropocentrism that fully envelops the visible space and the simple description of bodies, we have the emergence of a kind of *excavated anthropomorphism* for a visual site that becomes freed in order to be worked with: a site for inventing — in the archeological sense of the term: excavation in order to bring to the light of day — an unknown human form. A site for the emergence of the essential, namely the disturbingly strange. As in the case of the layered superposition of bodily cross-sections viewed from above, the skimming of which suddenly makes manifest, an undeniable and frontal, phantom of the human skull (fig. 12).

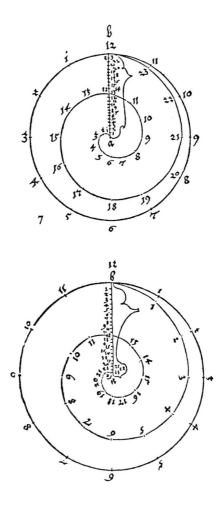

Fig. 7. Dürer, "The Spiral Line," *The Painter's Manual*, 50.
Fig. 8. "The Altered Spiral Line," ibid., 53.

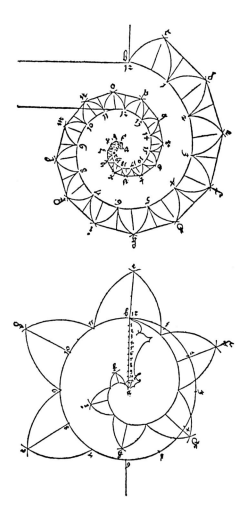

Fig. 9. "The Proper Length of Straight Lines Erected on a Spiral," ibid., 55.
Fig. 10. "This Line is Meant for a Bishop's Crozier," ibid., 57.

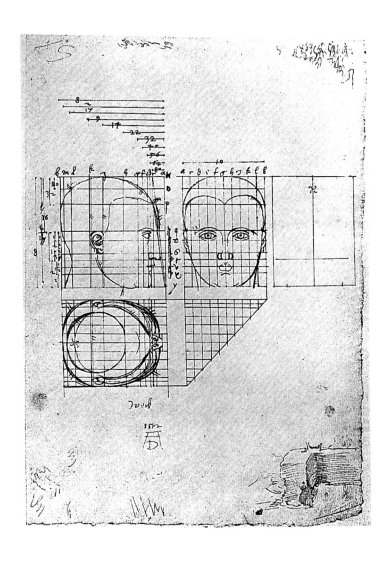

Fig. 11. Dürer, "The Head Constructed By Means of the 'Transfer' Method," *The Human Figure: The Complete Dresden Sketchbook*, edited by Walter Strauss (New York: Dover Publications, 1972), 220.

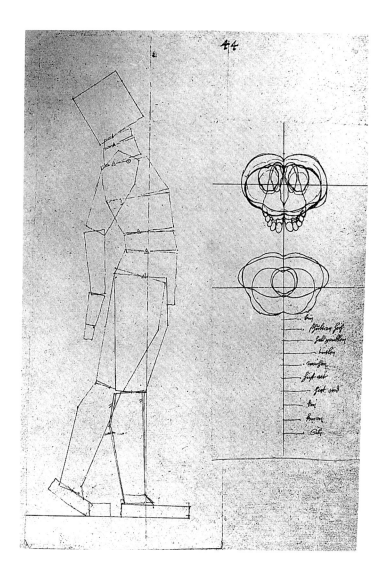

Fig. 12. "Stereometric Man: Two Body Sections," ibid., 202.

Être aître[11]

Aristotle believed the heart was the seat of thought. Then the head was graced with this honor. Galen assigned different mental functions to different regions of the brain.[12] But oh how it still remains difficult to think about (to imagine, to represent, to define, to even question) this *site of thought*! The inside of the head is, of course, invisible to us. As far as endogenous impressions and kinesthetic sensations are concerned, they remain rather impoverished and merely suggest to us, as the psychologists say, "a dome or cave" that we fill in with our visual images and autoscopic inventions.[13] For his part, Freud did quite a bit to propagate topical hypotheses of the psyche as well as archeological metaphors. He certainly knew how to reject any idealism (whether psychological or neo-Kantian) and how to refute any positivism (in particular of cerebral localizations); he certainly knew

---

11. I have chosen to keep the original French use of the word, *aître* in order to be faithful to the author's homophonic word play on the similarity between *être* and *aître*. Here *état d'aître*, state of *aître*, also no doubt references in its manner the more typically used phrase *état d'être*, or state of being. For more on the rapport between *être* and *aître* see p. 38 of the present chapter. [TN]

12. See Richard Broxton Onians, *The Origins of European Thought about the Body, the Mind, the Soul, the World, Time, and Fate* (Cambridge: Cambridge University Press, 1951).

13. See P. Solliers, *Les Phénomènes d'autoscopies* (Paris: Alcan, 1903), 45–75; Paul Schilder, *The Image and Appearance of the Human Body: Studies on the Constructive Energies of the Spirit* (New York: International Universities Press, 1950), 105–118; Bertram D. Lewin, *The Image and the Past* (New York: International Universities Press, 1968).

how to rethink thought — but, in the end, what did he discover if not the same, eternally cavernous [*béante*] question, the same enigma of the site of thought? "Space may be the projection of the extension of the psychical apparatus. No other derivation is probable. Instead of Kant's *a priori* determinants of our psychical apparatus. Psyche is extended; knows nothing about it."[14]

To know nothing about this site: so be it. But how does it *take* hold of us, how does it affect us, touch us? Artists don't provide us with any answers to these kinds of questions. At the very least, by way of displacing their points of view, by inverting spaces, by inventing new forms of relations and new contacts, *they incarnate the most essential questions*, which is indeed better than believing themselves capable of answering them.

Dürer, for example, provided a striking version of this non-knowledge and this united contact. His representation of Saint Jerome (figs. 13–14) develops a powerful trajectory — but such a paradoxical and reversible [*réversif*] one — between a living skull, still brimming with the activity of thought, and a lifeless skull whose somber cavities are exhibited in the foreground of the painting. In front of us, the thinker's left hand is thus pointed at the *object of his thought*: it's called *being a skull — être crâne* —vanity, humanity reduced to an empty snail shell, an instant of the soul [*échappée d'âme*]. In the background, within the symmetry of the curve (the left shoulder) and a counter curve (the right hand), the thinker's hand is placed on the *site of his thought*: this is also called *being a skull — être crâne — la*

14. Sigmund Freud, "Findings, Ideas, Problems," in *The Standard Edition of the Complete Psychological Works of Sigmund Freud* vol. 23, trans. James Strachey (London: Hogarth Press, 1964), 300. Cf. the comments of Pierre Fédida, *Le Site de l'étranger: La situation psychanalytique* (Paris: PUF, 1995), 267–298.

tempe soucieuse — *the mindful temple* — the temple of his forehead, the site of ontological questioning, the search for God — wandering within what theologians, since Augustine, have called the "region of dissemblance" — and, in the end, melancholia.[15]

But there is more: in creating this network of the two hands in contact with the two skulls, what Dürer will have uncovered for us is the clear relation between the *tactile site* and the *site of thought*. In touching this object placed before him like a mystery for his own thought, the theologian is not ignorant and knows very well that the mystery must be understood starting from the between-two where he himself is found: for what is before him to question finds an answer in what can be seen behind him, namely the strangely "living," corporeal, incarnated crucifix which creates the background. It is not by chance that Saint Jerome's authority is regularly evoked when the question of the relation between the *skull* and *Calvary* is discussed.[16] We know that most painters represent the skull at the base of their depictions of the Crucifixion: because the ghost of man's sin floats within the sacrifice of God. And in this manner, this skull is generally viewed as the skull of Adam himself. It is the human chalice that collects the divine blood, the chalice of sin that collects the flux of its future redemption.[17] Above all, the skull is also the specific site [*lieu-dit*] of the Christic death: a skull toponym, the foundational site for an entire religion. It's a rock in the form of an emaciated head where the decision will be made to

---

15. Erwin Panofsky, *The Life and Art of Albrecht Dürer* (Princeton, NJ: Princeton UP, 1955), 211-213. E. Panofsky misunderstood the melancholic component of this representation of Saint Jerome; he was also content in contrasting the engraving of Saint Jerome with the engraving of *Melancholia I*, both of which date from 1514.

16. See notably Thomas Aquinas, *Summa Theologica* IIIa (1485) Q. 46, Art. 10.

17. See W. Staude, "Le Crâne-chalice au pied de la Croix," *La Revue des arts* IV (1954), 137–142.

Figs. 13–14. Albrecht Dürer, *Saint Jerome in Meditation*, 1521 (details). Oil on panel. Lisbon, Museu Nacional de Arte Antiga. Photos by G. Didi-Huberman.

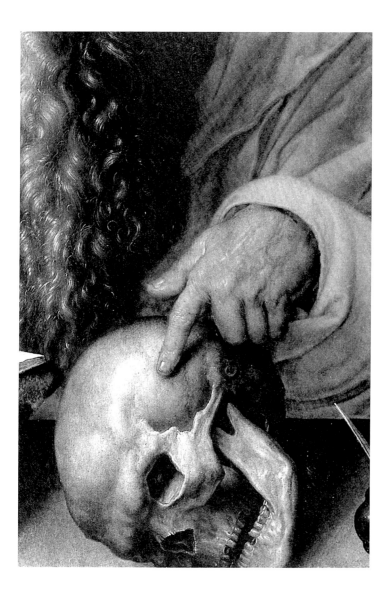

make a God die — *by contact*, and by contact I mean by way of the dilacerating blow of a lance upon Christ — in the image of man.[18]

Before the skull-sign, before the skull-object, there is therefore the *skull-site* — a site which worries thought and which nevertheless situates it, envelops it, touches it, and deploys it. Sites: anatomical excavations show them in abundance, from da Vinci to Vesalius, in whose work, for example, we can actually see the "map of cruelty" (much in the same way as one references the Map of Tendre[19]) of the cranial box (figs. 15–22). As far as our natural language is concerned, it expresses the skull-site just as fully as if the skull and brain were constituted of these specific sites, such as the "calotte," the "fountain," the "summit," the "rock," "tables," "pits," "cavities," "sutures," "holes," "canals," or "vaults" (as far as the cranium bone is concerned), "hemispheres," "aqueduct," "cistern," "pyramidal eminence," "isthmus," "pillars," or the "bridge of Varolius"(as far as the brain itself is concerned).

What kind of places are these? What do they do to our representation of space? The entire question resides here. Perhaps, in order to better grasp what is at stake, it would be better to evoke the anachronistic word *aître*, which, in French, has the phonetic particularity of turning the notion of *site* into a question concerning *being* — *être*. *Aître* first signified an *open space*, a porch, a passageway, an exterior churchyard (the etymology evokes the Latin *extera*); it is also used to signify a free and open terrain used for a charnel house or a

---

18. "Then delivered he him therefore unto them to be crucified. And they took Jesus, and led him away. And he bearing his cross went forth into a place called the place of a skull, which is called in the Hebrew Golgotha: Where they crucified him, and two other with him, on either side one, and Jesus in the midst." John XIX:16–18 (King James version).

19. The Map of Tendre was a map of an imaginary land created by a small group of individuals supposedly indicating the path toward love. [TN]

cemetery; it is also used to name the internal disposition of various parts of a habitat; it ended up signifying the intimacy of a being, his inner depths [*for intérieur*], the abyss itself of his thought.[20] When Henri Maldiney speaks of "*aîtres* of language" and of "dwellings for thought," he is first of all making a reference to the "nascent state" of language, of thought — this singularity that the poem, the work of art, proclaims each time.[21]

---

20. See P. Imbs, *Trésor de la langue française* II (Paris: Editions du CNRS, 1973), 401–402.

21. "The *aîtres* of language are, beyond its constructed state, the dwellings for a thought that has yet to be thematized into signs but whose powerful lucidity, instantaneous to all signs, founds, prior to any knowledge, the possibility itself of *signifying*. […] Only the poets still inhabit the *aîtres* of language, which are the foundation upon which the language of a poem, each time being singular, is built. […] The question regarding the relationship between language and thought can only be posed authentically by way of this *radical* level, where they each articulate each other in a *nascent state*." Henri Maldiney, *Aîtres de la langue et demeures de la pensée* (Lausanne: L'Age de l'homme, 1975), VII–IX.

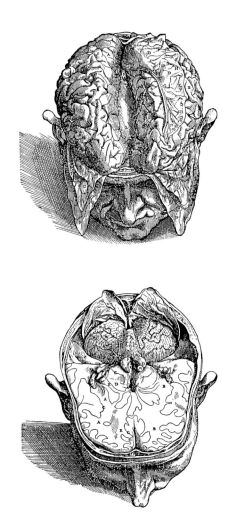

Figs. 15–22. Andreas Vesalius, *De Humani Corporis Fabrica* (Brussels, 1543), details of plates 7, 8, 48, 66, 67, 70, 71, 72.

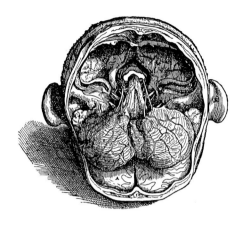

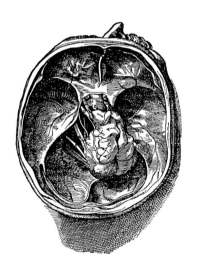

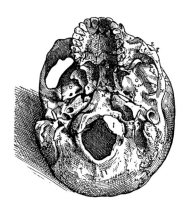

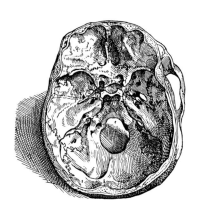

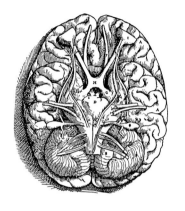

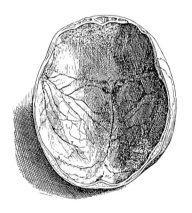

Being a River

Clearly, Giuseppe Penone is a sculptor of *aîtres* — his work becomes an interrogation of sites, and simultaneously one of being sculpted, being placed [*d'être posée*]. Which is to say, that from his hands, what emerges are not exactly objects, nor exactly sites. But rather *sites* produced in their "nascent state," in their visual and tactile state of *aître, state of being*.

But what should we understand by "*nascent state*?" Are we dealing with works that have been successfully achieved and exhibited in front of us as "finished," completed, and all in all, having reached an endpoint? To ask this question is to put one's finger on the difference between a sculpture which constructs objects in space — *objects of space*, we could say — and a sculpture which transforms objects into subtle actions of a site, into *taking or having place* [*avoir lieu*]. In the first case, the completed object exhibits its closure by affirming its results, by rejecting the agent and the action (the process whereby it takes form) of a single past, according to a kind of forgetting of its own birth. In the second case, the sculpture tends to remain open and instead affirms the entanglement or lack of separation [*inséparation*] it maintains between agent, action, and result. Each specific temporality of the work persisting within the others, enveloping them, and nourishing itself from them.

It is significant that Penone, in his method of writing and speaking about sculpture, always prefers verbal to substantive forms. It is significant that one of Penone's sculptures can have a verb as a title — an infinitive verb, so infinitely continuous, perhaps expressing an endless wish, unless it's a categorical imperative. So it is that from the verb "être" — to be — "being": the work entitled *Essere fiume* ("Being a River") offers itself up to be contemplated as a sculpture which, rightfully, with complete rigor, deploys the difference between the object and being, space and the *aître* (figs. 23–24). On one hand — but we don't know which one — there is the rock picked from a very precise site in the mountains that has been sculpted in the most traditional and humbly mimetic fashion that there is. On the other hand — but we will still remain unable to situate the hierarchy required by the usual notion of *mimesis* — the "model" of this object is found: it's a big rock taken from the river, at the foot of the mountain — a mass "naturally" formed by way of a very long duration of geological time where "stones strike against each other and break apart" and "the water washes away, carrying stone dust, polishes the material…." Indeed, according to Penone, such is the "process which tends to create forms,"[22] and this process is not a *mimesis*, but rather a material ontogenesis of form, a *dynamis* of the river itself. Most often, to make a sculpture is to make an *object*, to

22. Giuseppe Penone cited in Germano Celant's work, *Giuseppe Penone*, translated into French by Anne Machet (Milan/Paris: Electa-L. and Durand-Dessert, 1989), 21. In order to stay as close as possible to the source material referenced by the author, we have decided to provide the reader with translations of the various French versions of Penone's writings cited by Georges Didi-Huberman. For the interested reader who would like to further explore a larger collection of Giuseppe Penone's own writings in English translation, see *Giuseppe Penone: Writings 1968–2008*, edited by Gianfranco Maraniello and Jonathan Watkins (Bologna: Ikon Gallery and Bologna Museum of Modern Art, 2009). [TN]

carve out a material, to shape and form it, etc., then "finish" it, present it, exhibit it in public. So be it. But in the eyes of Penone it's above all to create within the intrinsic dynamic of the processes of formation, of physical morphologies where several secular polarities of aesthetic thought — art and nature, *technè* and *tuchè*, the organic and the geometrical — find themselves smashed together or more subtly linked, truly returned to their native entanglement.[23] As in the practices of Leonardo da Vinci, whose passion for rivers and the creative turbulence of forms we know rather well,[24] it's not the *natura naturata* (natural creation as a result of a process), but rather *natura naturans* (natural creation as a process in itself) which forms the essential stakes of artistic intention. Hence its anachronistic — hardly "modernist," even less "post-modern" — tone that we can denote in the quasi-pre-Socratic way which Penone has for looking at the river as a sculpture in full development.

The mutual collisions of the rocks during rising waters, the continuous rubbing of unsettled sand, the incessant movement of water on the bottom provoking the displacement of large stones, slow movements of medium-sized rocks, the more rapid current of loose stones, the accelerated flow of fine sand, a true river within the river.

The river transports the mountain. The river is the vehicle of the mountain. The blows, the shocks, the violent mutilations that the river inflicts on the biggest of rocks in colliding them with the smallest of stones, the infiltration of water within the thinnest of branches, within fissures, detaches pieces of the

23. See D. Soutif, "L'Identité retrouvée: la nature de l'art ou l'art de la nature," in *Giuseppe Penone* (Nantes: Musée des Beaux-Arts, 1986), 17–23. J-M Prévost, "Giuseppe Penone: l'oeuvre entre causalité et hasard," *Artstudio* 13 (1989), 120–135.

24. See Ernst H. Gombrich, "The Form of Movement in Water and Air," *The Heritage of Appelles: Studies in the Art of the Renaissance* (London: Phaidon, 1976), 39–56.

Figs. 23–24. Giuseppe Penone, *Essere fiume* [Being a river], 1981. Two stones, 50 x 33 x 30 cm. Photos courtesy G. Penone.

whole. Everything serves for sketching the form — the effect of a continuous work made by small and big blows, from the soft passage of sand, sharp ruptures, slow friction from great pressures, of muffled collisions. The form is sketched and becomes more and more apparent. Does the river not have as its project to reveal its essence to us, its purest and most secret quality, the extreme density of each element of the stone? [...]

It's impossible to imagine, impossible to work the stone according to a different mode than the one the river uses. A bradawl, a pin, a gradine, a chisel, an abrasive, sandpaper, are themselves tools of the river.

To extract a stone that the river has sculpted, to go backwards in the history of the river, to discover the exact place of the mountain from where the stone came, to extract the rock mass completely anew from the mountain, to reproduce within the mass the exact stone that was extracted from the river in the new block of stone, is to be the river oneself. [...] In order to truly sculpt a stone, one must be a river.[25]

In reading these — still wonderfully beautiful — excerpts from Penone,[26] it's easy to see the development, through biological processes and the materials of the physical world, a poetry or a poetics of the *natura naturans*. But it would be too easy, too reductive, to only see a vitalist effusion or fusion within landscape, a romanticism of the forest, ecologically aestheticized. Penone above all introduces us to his own practice; and yet, his practice is not that of some sort of agriculture, albeit a poetic one, but rather a *sculptura*

25. Penone, cited in Celant, 110.

26. For an excellent compendium of texts in French, the reader can explore the monograph by Celant, *Giuseppe Penone*. See also: Penone, "Mines," translated into French by F. M. Cattani, *Penone: l'espace de la main*, edited by R. Recht (Strasburg, Musées de la ville de Strasbourg, 1991), 193–198; Penone, *La structure du temps*, translated into French by F. Ferri (Annecy: DAO-La Petite École, 1993); and Penone, *L'Image du toucher*, translated into French by D. Ferault (Amiens: Fonds régional d'Art contemporain de Picardie, 1994).

sculpens, a sculpture which, endlessly, posits the question of its deployment with that of its "nascent state." When Penone affirms that being a sculptor is "being a river," he is above all making a comment on his singular choice of formal procedures.[27] He also develops a more general reflection on sculpture, where the network of poetic equivalence for which he has an affection,[28] more than anything else, refers to a veritable *temporal thought of sculpture* and of the specific places — of *aîtres* — they generate:

> For me, all the elements are fluid. The stone itself is fluid: a mountain crumbles, becomes sand. It is only a question of time. It's the short duration of our existence which leads us to deem a certain material as being either "hard" or "soft." Sculpture is founded upon the approach of a hard element and a soft element — in this case it's the chisel which penetrates into the wood. This is precisely what leads me to consider this aspect of things, in order to discern the issue.[29]

---

27. Also see Penone's piece: *Alpi Marittime. La mia altezza, la lunghezza delle mie braccia, il mio spessore in un ruscello* [Maritime Alps. My height, the length of my arms, my width in a stream], in *Writings 1968–2008*, 158–159.

28. Cf. J-L Baudry, "Le chemin des équivalences," *Giuseppe Penone* (Nantes: Musée des Beaux-Arts, 1986), 55–59.

29. Penone (1978) cited in Celant, 17. Penone, moreover, speaks of the contact of the hand with water, of the hand with plaster, as well as the body of the snake, which in his eyes is a sculptural contact in that it is both a "pocket and stick" and above all because "it proceeds from a vegetal and fluid logic." Penone, *La Structure du temps*, 35–40 and 125.

Being a Dig

So, how do we identify the problem? How does sculpture think? How does sculpture sculpt time? How does sculpture proceed along with this time itself — memory, present, protension toward the future — in order to disrupt our familiar spaces, that is, to disrupt our insides, to "touch" us with places, the *aîtres* that it invents? Here one must understand that the problematic of the "nascent state" has nothing nostalgic about it, nothing directed toward a thought origin [*origine pensée*] as the lost source of all things. *Essere fiume* is the clear proof of this, within the "dialectical image" that it offers of the encounter, in one and the same place, of two profoundly dissimilar temporalities (the geological time of the stone in the river, and the artistic time of the mountain).

It's when it erupts into the present, not as some distant source, but as the "eddy in the stream,"[30] as Walter Benjamin spoke of it in regard to the concept of origin — that the "nascent state" truly touches us. For example, we are indeed familiar with the idea, or the vague, idealized image, that our "site of birth" was the belly of our mother. But it is more difficult to familiarize ourselves with the present of

---

30. Walter Benjamin, *The Origins of German Tragic Drama*, trans. John Osborne (London: Verso, 1985), 45.

such a situation: it is difficult to wake up each morning and gaze into the mirror and see our own skull as a mold — an imprint hardened by our own years — of the mother's genital strait.[31]

And yet, it's precisely in this way that Penone succeeds in thinking the forms he invests in: sculpture thus takes on a value as *material anamnesis*, an anamnesis in action, in stone, in present time. Something else, assuredly, than the simple fabrication of a spatial object. When Penone sculpts, each gesture, each moment is produced within the coextension of things that are typically thought of as contradictory. Here, anamnesis takes the form of a kind of dialectical material: in this way, modeling [*modelage*] will be thought of by Penone as casting [*moulage*] (even when the entirety of classical thought regarding sculpture vehemently considers these two processes as diametrically opposed to each other).[32] What's more, the form that presents itself from out of the material will be understood as a result of an excavation, an archeological dig. And, in its own turn, this result will be thought as a dialectics of the substrate, of the void and flesh which dig:

---

31. "In normal love only a few characteristics survive which reveal unmistakably the maternal prototype of the object-choice, as, for instance, the preference shown by young men for maturer women; the detachment of libido from the mother has been effected relatively swiftly. In our type, on the other hand, the libido has remained attached to the mother for so long, even after the onset of puberty, that the maternal characteristics remain stamped on the love-objects that are chosen later, and all these turn into easily recognizable mother-surrogates. The comparison with the way in which the skull of a newly born child is shaped springs to mind at this point: after a protracted labor it always takes the form of a cast of the narrow part of the mother's pelvis." Sigmund Freud, "A Special Type of Choice of Object Made by Men," in *The Standard Edition of the Complete Psychological Works of Sigmund Freud*, vol. 11, trans. James Strachey (London: Hogarth Press, 1957), 169. I [GDH] thank Marie Moscovici for reminding me of this text.

32. "Every inquiry into the supposed voids presupposes a fullness [*le plein*]. This fullness is the sculptor himself, since with his chisel, with his hands, he exerts the pressure which creates volumes. A vase can be seen as a substitute for the hands of the potter, as a sum of his finger prints, as a matrix capable of recreating (when one grasps the vase) the skin of the potter." Penone, cited in Celant, 85.

When one plunges one's hand into the ground in order to extract dirt, a void is created where the hand has passed: the earth becomes mixed, a sculpture takes form. The void of the flesh becomes earth.[33]

To make a sculpture? For Penone, this also becomes to do *a dig*. To make an anamnesis out of the material retained from where one has plunged one's hand: what the hand retains of the material is nothing other than a present form, in which all the singular *times of the site*, of which the material is made, from which it draws its "nascent state," are accumulated and inscribed. Thus, for the sculptor, memory is a quality proper to the material itself: *matter is memory*. Utilizing coal — even if it is merely a little piece of a charcoal stick — Penone will question himself concerning the troubling fact that carbon provides the most stable element of the difference between plant, animal, and mineral life. The memory of carbon will cross paths with that of the artist so that a material image of the "nascent state" of the mineral emerges — this image is nothing less than the decomposition of animal bodies, even human bodies, immemorially layered in the earth, agglutinated into peat and coal:

> How is coal born? There is a crowd. We are so cramped, packed together, that we smother each other, we doggedly struggle for more space, crammed, pressed, trampled upon, we flatten ourselves, we smash ourselves, we compress ourselves, reduce ourselves, penetrate ourselves, and in this way, by way of a twisting movement [*en un mouvement de torsion*], we extract the light from out of ourselves; pressed, hardened, mutually penetrated, we become matter, solid matter but from which emanates the stench of fear. [...] A stratification of men, who become dust, earth, the eyelid hiding the eye from the

33. Ibid., 27, see also 92 and 140.

full view of occurred things. To succeed in seeing the eye of the earth.[34]

But the sculptor must invest in all the meanings [*sens*] of time. To dig is not merely to hollow out the earth in order to extract from it things that have long since died. It's also to conserve [*ménager*], within the opened earth — *œuvrée, ouvrée: worked, opened*, as it was once said — a passage where forms themselves have a memory of their own becoming, of their birth or future growth. It will suffice for Penone to create, within the earth, the intimate embrace of a counter-form (or rather the embrace of a *form* in the primary sense, which is the *negative*) of the earth's head and its vegetal seeding (pumpkins or potatoes), in order for the sculptor's *head at the nascent state* to be capable of slowly seeing the the light of day starting from a place other than the maternal belly (figs. 25–26). The archeology of material here does not happen without the archeology of a subject which confronts itself: thus, would not the art of the sculptor consist of digging out galleries, of excavating the memory of his own flesh and thought? We will not be surprised to learn that Penone has made his work according to the hypothesis of a descent into "the mines of the skull":

> We descend into the brain by way of vertical wells which take us into diverse depths; at each stop, galleries lead, by way of reasoning, to the excavation of ideas; once they have been detected, they are brought up to the surface; and the more the brain is rich in memory sediments, the more galleries there are, the more stops, the more excavations [*fronti di scavo*].[35]

---

34. Penone, "Mines," 195–197; see also *La structure du temps*, 11.
35. Penone, "Mines," 193; see also *La structure du temps*, 5.

Figs. 25–26. Penone, *Potatoes*, 1977. Photographic documentation by Garessio. Photos courtesy of G. Penone.

Being a Fossil

Envisioned spontaneously, excavation offers a rather trivial image of thought. Is it enough to say that we "scratch our head," and that we then look "to extract an idea from out of it" in order to account for the *aîtres* of thought? Certainly not. But Penone produced this image merely as a working hypothesis; the work itself would be to *sculpturally* deploy and shape — that is, to push to their most unexpected and reversive tactile limits — images of the dig, of depth, of interiority. Here, it's the task of the sculpture itself *to touch thought*.

Penone takes a skull in his hands, opens it, and looks at it. Beyond any metaphysical or religious anxieties — like those belonging to Dürer, for example — beyond any anatomical curiosities — like those belonging to da Vinci, for example — Penone will question, scrutinizing the interior of this skull, a kind of tactile blindness which we rarely reflect upon: our brain is in contact with an internal face [*paroi*] which it knows nothing about, that it doesn't see, and that it doesn't even feel (to paraphrase Freud, we could say that the "psyche is in contact, and doesn't know it"). How, then, do we re-establish to this unknown contact — which is nevertheless intrinsic to the "dwellings of thought" — its capacity for ontological worry, its possible truth effect *concerning us*? The answer is sculpture, namely, a technical hypothesis carefully explored, deployed, and incarnated. Onto the limestone-covered cranial face, Penone places a graphite powder — the choice of material will not surprise us, in such a context — and continues with a delicate *frottage* of microscopic reliefs, networks, and veins, of the surface. This texture will be harvested via a transparent adhesive tape, which is itself used, by way of four zones which cover the internal surface of the cranial box, as an optical and projective tool (basically, as a kind of tactile photographic slide). The result is a mural: four large panels that, exposed within a closed off site, develop, by way of a precise transfer, the blind contact of a brain with its skull (figs. 27–30). As if our brain was capable of turning itself into a hand, of caressing its own matrixial gangue.

> The instrument for touching is the hand, the epidermis of hands. Our body's sensory receptors are above all located on the surface and not on the inside.
>
> Our body is composed of hard and soft parts. The cranial box, the hard protection of the skull, is adapted to the form it protects. The cranial bone is a plastic material for the brain that constructs the bone and adapts it to the brain's form. The brain adheres to the skull in which it registers its pulses, but it is not capable of reading the surface that it touches. In order to understand the form of the internal surface of the skull and to take it into account, one must touch it with one's hands, see it with one's own eyes. Once again, we have an image by way of the intermediary of *frottage*: an extreme *frottage* produced within the interior of the skull.[36]

---

36. Penone, *L'Image du toucher*, 6–7.

What's surprising is that, after having dispensed with geological metaphors for the very precise and direct procedure of *frottage*, the artist obtains a result whose visual quality is still — and irrefutably so — that of an *excavation site*. As we know, *frottage* is an archeological technique par excellence: it captures the most ancient and least visible of traces that there are. Revealing *fossils of gestures*: brief time periods (the passage of animals) or long time periods (geological formations) that have become hardened and compressed like charcoal. And yet, for Penone, to be a sculpture is also to be a fossil: an imprint of time, whose specific space — or what I would like to call instead: its site, its *aître* — inverts or reverses all of our familiar orientations, paradoxically rendering the possibility of developing the intimacy of a gesture or a contact.

> Space precedes us. Space preceded our ancestors. Space will continue after us. To fossilize gestures most certainly or probably realized at a certain place reduces the possible usage of the space but also marks the space itself. […] To create a sculpture is a vegetal gesture; it's the trace, it's the process, the power of adherence, the fossil of the completed gesture, immobile action, a waiting [*une attente*], a point of life and death.[37]

Is it a question of sculpture? A question of *aître* and of fossil: the becoming-time of place, the becoming-place of time. And, as a consequence, a question of sediments, of interstices, of contacts. Is sculpture the site where we touch time?

> How does time pass? To speak to a stone or dig up a mind [*creuser un esprit*]. In digging up a stone does it speak to the

---

37. Penone, cited in Celant, 116 and 158.

Figs. 27–30. Penone, *Landscape of the Brain*, 1990. Charcoal on adhesive ribbon. Photos courtesy of G. Penone.

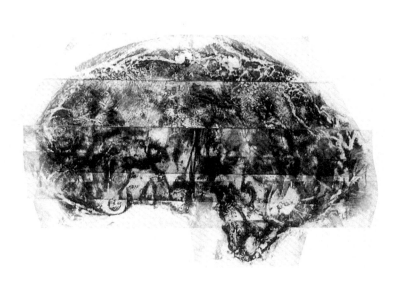

mind? […] Does the problem then become once again one of space? It's by way of space that we harvest the value of time, the memories of time; space can be the void between the fingernail and the flesh, a void which becomes filled with dirt.

It could also be the void between the brain and the skull, the space of the sculpture, that fills in with charcoal powder. What then does this rubbed space, this space that is "*frotté,*" fossilize? What do its reticulations, its meningeal networks, tell us? Anthropologists and paleontologists based their reconstitutions of cephalic development of hominids around observable meningeal networks found within the *imprints* left on the interior face of pre-historic skulls. Roger Saban, notably, developed the notion of the *brain fossil*: by returning to the practice of endocranial casting — once used only as the means for calculating cephalic volume — he was able to establish a new "paleoneurology," by way of deducing these meningeal images, whose stakes were none other than the phylogeny itself of human language: the emergence, throughout the long duration of the species, of a cerebral organization authorizing "the nascent state" of our articulated language (figs. 31–34).[38]

Would sculpture be a site where we become capable of touching thought or a language yet to be born?

---

38. See Roger Saban, *Anatomie et évolution des veines méningés chez les hommes fossiles* (Paris: ENSB-CTHS, 1984); and *Aux sources du langage articulé* (Paris: Masson, 1993), 169–229.

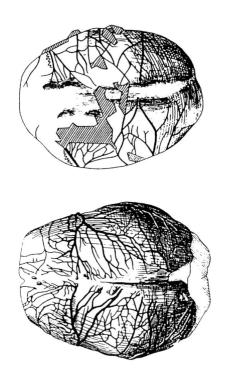

Figs. 31–34. Meningeal veins of type sapiens on intercranial casts of pre-
historic skulls. After Roger Saban, *Aux sources du langage articulé*, 206.

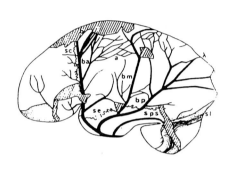

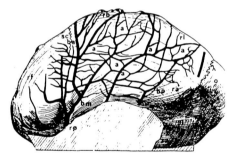

Being a Leaf

But to touch is not to grasp, even less to possess or to master. If Penone's work indeed comes from the *arte povera* movement, as it is said, then one must understand within this "poverty" a sharp theoretical awareness that *sculpture works with traces* rather than with objects. Sculpture's object itself would be that of the trace in the dual sense of vestige and "nascent state": "the point of life and the point of death," as Penone himself so aptly put it. As for the impression — created by the *frottage* technique — it would perhaps designate this necessary heuristic and technical dimension wherein the sculptural concern for *working the traces* is deployed.

The impression is humble. It retains, it reports. In actualizing his *frottages*, works of patience and submission to the already traced forms, Penone has, he says, the feeling of effectuating a "reading" of things: both a blind and comprehensive reading, a close, productive, tactile reading of an intimate knowledge — but even to do this, we must be deprived of our habitual distance to our objectivations.[39] One must choose how one wants to know: either one wants

---

39. "A *frottage* is just as much a reading and a comprehension as it is a faithful recording of form. It is an immediate and direct image, the first image of reality, the first reading and codification of a surface. An action of knowledge through the skin [...]." Penone, *L'Image du toucher*, 4.

a ("objective") point of view, and then one must distance oneself and not touch; or one wants (sensual) contact, and then the object of knowledge becomes a material that envelops us, releasing us from ourselves, leaving us with no positive certainty whatsoever. In realizing, starting in 1978, his *frottages* of eyelids — using a technique similar to the one he used for the skull (figs. 35–36) — Penone indicates to what extent the decision of imprinting, for him, always refers back to a sort of *tactile immersion within the place*:

> The image is formed by pressure. I projected the obtained image, repeating it in order to constitute a series of actions, a series which completely enveloped me. However, it wasn't an image that was found elsewhere. It was my body that created it, and I created the gesture for touching. A banal and insignificant action, worthless. What's more, when I looked back over the image once again, I didn't trust in any of my projections. As I advanced, I learned more about my body than about the surface of the wall. It was as if I was walking upon my own skin, which was also a manner of walking upon the skin of space.[40]

Between "me" and "space," there is nothing but skin. It is a receptacle, an imprint-bearer of the world around me that sculpts me. At the same time, it's an excavation site of my destiny — of the time that sculpts me. And in the end, it's a writing of my flesh, an ensemble of traces that emit, from the interior of my skull, an unconscious thought — a thought which also sculpts me. Skin is a paradigm: lining, bark, leaf, eyelid, fingernail, or the shedding of a snake, it's toward skin, toward *knowledge by way of contact*, that a large

---

40. Penone, cited in Celant, 20. Cf. as well ibid., 64: "A *frottage* of the tree branches and trunks, of the blades of grass, of the leaves and the bark. [...] Capturing the green of the forest. To traverse in one gesture the green of the forest. To efface the green of the forest. To add back into the forest the green of the forest itself."

part of the sculptural phenomenology at work in Penone seems to orient itself around. Skin-limit or skin-pocket, skin-division, or skin-immersion, blind skin or a deciphering skin of forms — all these motives can be found unremittingly traversing the work of the artist.[41]

Would being a sculpture thus also mean being skin? More specifically, it would perhaps be a skin capable of granting everything it touches the relative permanence of its imprints. And yet, when we touch something with our hand, the exact place where contact is made becomes invisible to us (we have to remove our hand in order to see what we are touching). Such is the paradox specific to image-contacts, which produce their visuality itself within the event of a *blind* take [*prise aveugle*]:

> The adhesion, the connection of the tool with the earth, the pressure, everything is a part of creating the image. At that moment, the skin is hidden from view, all that remains is a tactile reading, by way of contact, and which thus presents an image of pressure. The skin has completely disappeared by way of the action of adhesion which creates the image. The skin at once becomes fashioned and also fashions itself; all this is dependent upon elasticity, density, and flexibility as well as the ability of the material to remember.[42]

Here we can understand how *frottage* can even appear as being beyond — the "beyond of painting" that Max Ernst hoped for — as a sculptural process *par excellence*.[43]

---

41. See notably ibid., 58, 60, 104; Penone, *La Structure du temps*, 9, 44, 50, 63, 115; *L'Image du toucher*.

42. Penone, cited in Celant, 104.

43. See Max Ernst, *Beyond Painting, and Other Writings by the Artist and His Friends* (Chicago: Solar Books, 2009), 235–269.

Figs. 35–36. Penone, *Eyelids*, 1978. Charcoal on canvas, 1000 x 200 cm. Photographic documentation by Garessio. Photos courtesy of G. Penone.

Since, thanks to the interface of sensitive skin, it is capable of transforming one volume into another, such as the shrub on which Penone performed a *frottage* and which filled up the entire volume of a small book. The network of poetic equivalences that are dear to the artist — lining, bark, leaf, eyelid, fingernail, or snake sheddings — are here revealed in their formal and processual aspects of *topical conversions*. This is not by way of the play of metaphor but rather by way of the force of morphology that Penone convinces us of the vegetal character of his eyelids or the cerebral character of simple leaf from a tree (figs. 37–38):

> The Leaves of the brain. Closed eyelids, the exact definition of limits and space, of thought, reflect the notion of our body in space.
>
> Closed eyelids, definition of the plenitude of sculpture pitted against the void of sight.
>
> Closed eyelids, cerebral hemispheres, thought matter.
>
> Closed eyelids, isolation, islands of sight.
>
> Closed eyelids, definition of the sub-soil, traversal of the sub-soil, sediment of dust.
>
> Closed eyelids, annotation of space.[44]

Skin, eyelids, cervical envelopes: each one of them is nothing other than the limit-case of the other, according to the spatial logic which can't be thought of without calling to mind da Vinci's onion. And all of them will be seen by Penone as so much bark and leaves — the leaves themselves

---

44. Penone, *La Structure du temps*, 67.

seen as "the air's skin"[45] — since everything proceeds from the same *dynamis*, from the same kind of morphogenetic law. This is why Penone's work can principally be understood as the *development* of forms. *Visual development*, in the first sense that the verb "develop" has, which is that of "making appear": to dis-envelop what was enveloped or to stretch out that which was rolled up (here we can even think of algebraic development, which brings to the light of day, through a series or a function, all the different terms that it contains; we can think of geometrical development, which allows us to visualize on a plane the diverse sides of one and the same volume). *Temporal development*, in the second meaning that this term takes on, the term of the "nascent state" and process of growth. It is probable that Penone sees with the help of the fingerprint, within the tactile knowledge that the print authorizes, a way of "developing" which is not simply visual (the projection to the outside of an endocranial *frottage*), but also temporal: as if, from then on being visible on the four walls of the architectural space, the meningeal networks of an expired thought continued to call for a response in summoning our gazes, our words, our thoughts.

---

45. "The leaves, the air's skin, the negative of the wind, sculpted and shaped by the wind, elements created in the air by the air, leaves which tend to occupy the peaceful interstices, the smallest of nooks. As soon as they lose their flexible fibers and become an obstacle for the wind, they are grasped, ripped up, carried off into the air. Dry, they curl up, dwindle, and become tightly wound. They then resemble a spiral, a shell, a snail's shell, wind horns. Pressing its skin against the air." Ibid., 119.

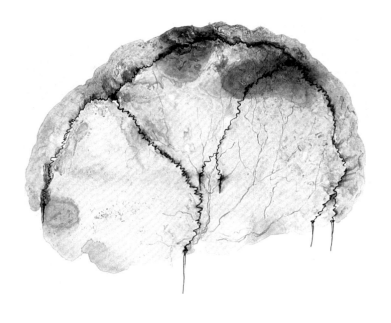

Fig. 37. Penone, *Landscape of the Brain*, 1990. Vinegar and ink on paper. Photo courtesy of G. Penone.

Fig. 38. Penone, *Leaves of the Brain*, 1986. Graphite and charcoal on Bristol board, 32.8 x 47.8 cm. Photo courtesy of G. Penone.

Being a Site

"Leaves of the brain," "closed eyelids," "annotation of space": sculpture would thus take on the value of skin in that it would be capable of developing (by way of contact, *frottage*, projective relation) a spatiality that visual experience generally remains unable to grasp, to grab hold of. What strange space, what sort of site are we then dealing with?

First of all, it's a *site for getting lost* — a "path that leads nowhere." It's a site where we must tread carefully, where we must feel our way along, via tactility, because we are not able to predict the various forks in the path. It's a rhizome, something that evokes the vegetal reticulations of a tuber, of a piece of bark, of a leaf, mineral galleries of an archeological dig, the capillary vessels of my own eyelids, the sutures found on my own skull (figs. 35–40). To sculpt, according to Penone, is to take off on the "disappeared trail," to renounce predictable forms in order to rediscover a pathway within the lack of evidence of the formless material: "To find a pathway, to traverse it, to probe it by clearing away the brush, this is sculpture."[46]

---

46. Penone, cited in Celant, 154.

Figs. 39–40. Penone, *Sutures*, 1987-1990 (details). Steel, plexiglass, and clay, 350 x 400 x 370 cm. Photos by Gérard Rondeau.

Next, it's a *site for losing space* — in order to refute it, to invert it at the drop of a hat, turning its usual coordinates upside down. If the skull is a sculptural object *par excellence*, it's not simply because, when placed at a "presentable" distance, its forms are beautiful to study or because its volumes are interesting to represent.[47] The skull is a sculptural object for the more essential and organic reason that our brain is incapable of imagining its true spatiality — the "cradled ceiling" [*le plafond en berceau*] offering nothing more for our representation than a convenient and culturally reproducible substitute.[48] And yet, the fingerprint appears to be the most appropriate material process for visually recognizing such a paradox: the *frottage* of the meningeal networks (figs. 27–30) at the same time offers a *development*, an exact relation of the endocranial relief, as well as a *reversal* of their — inaccessible — spatial coordinates. In front of these works, the sensation of place emerges from out of such a reversal: the sensation of place envelops us within invisible space like a landscape, which because of this fact then haptically envelops [*environne*] our brain, within the blind gangue of our cranial bone.

> It's a veritable landscape, with depressions, riverbeds, mountains, plateaus, a relief identical to the earth's crust. The landscape which surrounds us, we also possess it inside this projection box. It's the landscape inside which we think, the landscape which envelops us. A landscape to traverse, to feel, to know through touching, to draw point by point, like a

---

47. See notably, Henry Moore, *Elephant Skull* (Geneva: G. Cramer, 1970).

48. See Penone, cited in Celant, 156: "As the brain needs space, incapable as it is to imagine itself in its real space, in particular when man feels anxiety when inside spaces with flat ceilings. For the reason that the idea itself of thought, and the reclamation of thought reclaims a cradled ceiling. This is no doubt the reason why, in the past, figurative sculpture was inserted under arches, inside alcoves, and at the bottom of awnings."

blind person feels around with his cane in order to decipher the space that surrounds him.[49]

The imprint develops and the imprint reverses. It can also develop organically starting from itself, that is to say, by inverting itself, perpetually reversing itself. Thus, Penone did not simply stop at the process of *frottage*: he began to mold and shape, developing and repeating the operation several times, and he ended up forming a kind of immense onion where the gangues became superimposed, the "virtual" skins of the brain in metamorphosis (figs. 41–46). In sculpting this, Penone obviously turns space upside down. One thinks of an igloo in plaster — in any case, it's a *dwelling*. It's a site *par excellence*, which teaches us what an "*aître*" or a "dwelling" means: a dwelling would not be that which we inhabit, but *that which simultaneously inhabits and incorporates us.*

49. Penone, *L'Image du toucher*, 7.

Figs. 41–46. Penone, *The Tree of Vertebrae*, 1996. Photos courtesy G. Penone.

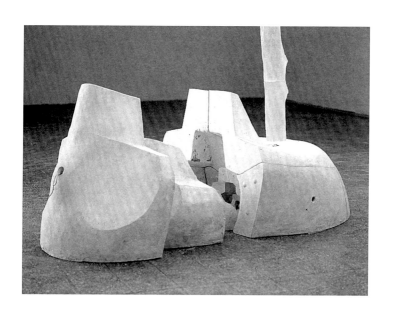

Figures

The Groove of the Poem: Reading Philippe Beck
Jacques Rancière

A careful reading of one of France's most important contemporary poets by one of today's most engaging thinkers of aesthetics.

Grafts: Writings on Plants
Michael Marder

A vital call for the cross-pollination of philosophy and plant sciences.

A Love of UIQ
Félix Guattari

An exciting attempt by one of France's most well known thinkers wherein he explores his thought through the form of a cinematic narrative.

Desert Dreamers
Barbara Glowczewski

An ethnographic adventure exploring the Warlpiri and their cultural practices of "the dreaming" in relation to their societal laws, ritual art, and connection with the cosmos.

Cartography of Exhaustion: Nihilism Inside Out
Peter Pál Pelbart

A meditation on the possibility of fighting off the exhaustion of our contemporary age of communicative and connective excess.

Other Univocal Titles

Univocal Publishing
411 N. Washington Ave, Suite 10
Minneapolis, MN 55401
www.univocalpublishing.com

ISBN 9781937561703

Jason Wagner, Drew S. Burk
(Editors)
All materials were printed and bound
in August 2016 at Univocal's atelier
in Minneapolis, USA.

This work was composed in Adobe Garamond
The paper is Hammermill 98.
The letterpress cover was printed
on Crane's Lettra Fluorescent.
Both are archival quality and acid-free.